Famous Friends:

Henry Ford
AND
Thomas Edison

*How They Met, Their Humble Beginnings
and Amazing Achievements*

John Bankston

CURIOUS
FOX
BOOKS

ABOUT THE AUTHOR: Although John Bankston has written dozens of biographies on everyone from Stephen Hawking to Jennifer Lawrence, this is the first time he has taken a look at two people and how their friendship affected their lives. If you've every turned on a light in a dark room or gone on a car trip, you can thank Edison and Ford. Yet, the two changed the world in ways we probably don't realize. Bankston lives in Miami Beach, Florida, and was very interested in how the two men helped develop Fort Myers—a place where his parents once had a winter home.

© 2024 by Curious Fox Books™, an imprint of Fox Chapel Publishing Company, Inc., 903 Square Street, Mount Joy, PA 17552.

Famous Friends: Henry Ford and Thomas Edison is a revision of *Famous Friends: True Tales of Friendship: Henry Ford and Thomas Edison*, published in 2020 by Purple Toad Publishing, Inc. Reproduction of its contents is strictly prohibited without written permission from the rights holder.

PUBLISHER'S NOTE: This story has not been authorized by the estates of Henry Ford or Thomas Edison.

Paperback ISBN 979-8-89094-012-4
Hardcover ISBN 979-8-89094-013-1

Library of Congress Control Number: 2023952422

To learn more about the other great books from Fox Chapel Publishing, or to find a retailer near you, call toll-free 800-457-9112 or visit us at *www.FoxChapelPublishing.com*.

We are always looking for talented authors. To submit an idea, please send a brief inquiry to acquisitions@foxchapelpublishing.com.

Fox Chapel Publishing makes every effort to use environmentally friendly paper for printing.

Printed in China

CONTENTS

Chapter 1
Unlikely Savior 5

Chapter 2
The Wizard 11

Edison Invents the Music Business 19

Chapter 3
Human Machines 21

Ford, Studebaker, DeLorean . . . Tesla 27

Chapter 4
Friends and Neighbors 29

Florida Real Estate 33

Chapter 5
Remembrance 35

Going Electric 39

Chronology 40

Chapter Notes 42

Further Reading 44

Glossary 47

Index 48

By 1914, Thomas Edison was a successful movie producer, overseeing dozens of motion pictures at his New Jersey facility and in this Bronx studio.

CHAPTER 1

Unlikely Savior

The fire spread quickly. An explosion just after sunset ignited reels of film like so much gunpowder, shattering every window in the two-story structure. Carried by an eastern wind, sparks settled on a neighboring building, setting it ablaze. Soon at least ten buildings were engulfed. Thomas Edison watched them burn.

In the West Orange, New Jersey, facility, Edison had been experimenting with movies and recorded sound. By that night in December 1914, the lab and its contents were worth over seven million dollars. "I'd just gone home for dinner when they sent for me to hurry back to the plant," Edison told author James Draper Newton. "When I got there, everything except the main laboratory and the library was in flames. There was nothing I could do but watch." By then, firefighters from West Orange and the surrounding towns had arrived to battle the blaze. They were powerless against the inferno. Edison's son Charles was also there. "I said to him, 'Get mother and her friends over here. They'll never see a fire like this again,'" Edison recalled.[1]

Mina Edison took charge during the 1914 fire, with little thought for her own safety.

Mina Edison did more than watch. She helped others rescue vital papers from the company's office. They stopped only when that building also caught fire.

Speaking to a reporter, the elderly inventor was optimistic. "Although I am over 67 years old, I'll start again tomorrow. . . . There will be a mobilization here and the debris will be cleared away. . . . I will go right to work to reconstruct the plant."[2]

Edison's optimism was misplaced. He aggressively protected his inventions, suing anyone who copied them. He had been less careful protecting his property. He told Newton he "never understood the humbuggery of bookkeeping. I kept only payroll accounts. I hung a record of payments on one hook and one of expenses on another hook . . . [when a large bill] was due, I'd hustle to raise the money."[3]

Edison realized that just replacing the property would take every penny he had. He probably felt like the desperate young man he'd once been, back when he was broke and hungry and trying to make it big.

Early the next morning, thousands of Edison's employees reported to work. Most joined the salvage crew. Well-educated engineers and technicians worked beside the laborers—all of them digging through the rubble for anything that could be saved.

Charles Edison spent much of his life working beside his famous father.

By then, car manufacturer Henry Ford had heard the news and was on his way from Detroit. When he arrived at West Orange, he "didn't say much, just handed me a check," Edison told Newton. "You'll need some money," Ford said, adding, "Let me know if you need more." Edison looked at the check. "It was made out for $750,000! He didn't ask for any security and of course over the years I repaid the principle but he never would take a cent of interest."[4]

It was an incredible amount of money in 1914. That year, workers lined up for blocks to earn five dollars a day at Ford's auto plant. That salary was twice what other factories were paying. Working nonstop, it would have taken one of them over 400 years to earn what Ford had handed to Edison. Then again, Edison was a big reason Ford was a multimillionaire.

In 1914, Ford's company was selling the world's most popular automobile, making Ford one of the richest men in the world.

In this 1924 photograph, Henry Ford looks upon the first Model T his company sold, while the ten millionth sits behind him. By then, the car's sales were declining because he refused to develop new models.

Edison started as Ford's mentor, offering advice and encouragement. The two became close friends. They often spent winters in a Florida neighborhood named after the inventor.

Still, Edison and Ford were very different. Ford seemed to go without stopping, while Edison could sit quietly and think. In fact, he often went fishing, hoping the hobby would keep people from asking him questions. Newton learned that Edison sometimes didn't even bait his hook. He didn't want the fish to break his train of thought either!

Still, when Edison was asked a question, he didn't hesitate. Bob Halgrim worked for him as a teenager. He was in his 90s when he told a reporter, "If you asked Mr. Ford a question, he'd say, 'I'll tell you tomorrow,' and then he'd get the ideas of the people who worked for him. But if you asked Mr. Edison a question, he'd give you his opinion right off."[5]

Despite their differences, they had much in common. They hated laziness. They believed success came to anyone who worked hard and didn't quit. And they both grew up in the Midwest, learning most of what they knew not in a classroom but at their mother's knee.

Even though the 1914 fire destroyed most of Edison's factory and operation, Building Number 5, also known as the Battery Factory, survived the fire with little damage due to its durable cement walls. Edison's Battery Factory building still stands today and has been converted to an apartment building known as Edison Lofts.

Long before he was a famous inventor, Thomas Edison was a hardworking boy who never seemed to have just one job.

CHAPTER

The Wizard

2

Thomas Edison grew up watching his father fail. Samuel Edison ran a grocery store and sold real estate in the Midwest. He built a tower for tourists to climb and admire the view. His businesses usually went out of business. Yet, Samuel didn't give up.

Historian Paul Israel believes, "This sent a very positive message to his son—that it's okay to fail—and may explain why he rarely got discouraged if an experiment didn't work out."[1]

When Thomas Alva Edison was born on February 11, 1847, his parents, Nancy and Samuel, already had six children. Often, the "baby" of the family is spoiled or ignored, but Thomas experienced neither. Although the Edison home in Milan, Ohio, was crowded, his parents made time for their children. Being a former schoolteacher, Nancy taught Thomas at home. Like his father, Thomas did not do well in school, but they both loved books.

When Thomas was seven, the family moved to Port Huron, Michigan. At age 12, Thomas got his first job. He sold newspapers and candy to passengers on the Grand Trunk Railroad, which ran between Port Huron and Detroit. He soon took over a baggage car, printing a paper of his own.

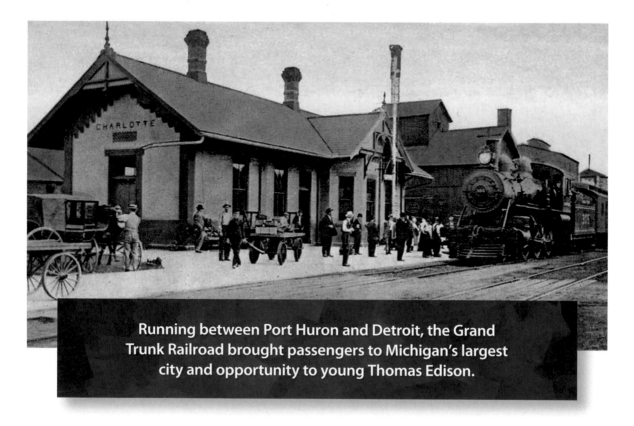

Running between Port Huron and Detroit, the Grand Trunk Railroad brought passengers to Michigan's largest city and opportunity to young Thomas Edison.

He was the *Weekly Herald*'s sole reporter, editor, and publisher. Soon it had dozens of subscribers paying eight cents a month.

Thomas made the most of the train's Detroit layover. He'd spend the hours in the local library there, reading about the telegraph.

Instant Communication

Although others figured out how to send messages via wires, Samuel F.B. Morse's invention changed communication. Other systems used multiple wires and needles. His needed a single overhead electrical wire connected to the ground. When an electromagnet in the receiver broke the circuit, it made a short or long "click"—a dot or a dash. Morse grouped these dots and dashes in various ways to make letters and numbers: *Morse code.*

Like a twenty-first-century teen learning computer code, Thomas taught himself Morse code. It helped him get a good-paying job in a press office, recording news that had been wired from far away.

At a young age, Thomas was losing his hearing, which was speculated to be from either an illness or injury. Thomas never complained, saying it let him sleep better. It also kept him from being distracted in the busy press office, where the only telegraph he could hear was his own.

At 21, he moved to Boston, Massachusetts. Since telegraph operators also had to repair

Like many successful inventors, Samuel F.B. Morse drastically improved an existing technology rather than discovering something completely new.

equipment, he learned a lot about electricity. He knew how batteries worked and how to wire circuits. His first patent was for an electrical vote recorder that used telegraph technology to record votes. The Massachusetts legislature wasn't interested. At the time, votes were written down in the presence of politicians making speeches.

This didn't discourage Edison and he decided to make a career for himself as an inventor.

In 1874, Edison developed the quadruplex telegraph system. Instead of sending one message over the wire, it could send up to four (two each way). When he brought it to the Western Union Telegraph Company, its value was obvious. When asked how much he wanted, Edison was about

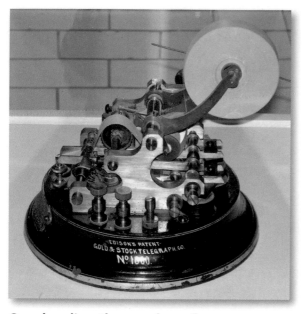

Quadrupling the number of messages a telegraph can send and receive helped make young Thomas Edison a rich man.

to suggest $2,000. Then he had a better idea: he said, "Well suppose you make me an offer." They offered him $40,000! It was an incredible amount of money for the time.[2]

Edison claimed that he cashed the check and stuffed his pockets with money. Although he might have made that part up, he put the cash to good use, buying buildings near the Menlo Park, New Jersey, train station.

Edison is best remembered for the things he invented. Yet, his biggest invention might have been the *way* those things were created. He opened an "invention factory." It employed the brightest scientists alongside skilled craftsmen who had access to the best materials. There, they worked on developing many of Edison's ideas. No one had worked this way before, but the modern campuses of Google and Apple resemble Edison's Menlo Park.

By this time, Edison was a husband and a father. He had married Mary Stillwell, a 16-year-old who worked for him, in 1871. The couple had three children, but neither Mary, Marion, Thomas, Jr., nor William saw much of their husband or father. Edison worked 16 hours at a time, became known for not sleeping, and took naps wherever he could, such as under a bush, on his workbench, or on a cot in the back of the lab. When he was a newlywed, he complained in his diary that his new wife still hadn't invented anything.

In 1876, Alexander Graham Bell introduced his telephone. Unfortunately, the design did not work over long distances. The next year, Edison, with help from Charles Batchelor, invented a transmitter that used a carbon button to greatly extend its range. It improved the phone so much that his design endured for the next 100 years.

While inventors like Bell had long tried to record sound, Edison beat them. As Edison tried to record Morse code, he realized that sound vibrated. Perhaps his deafness gave him greater insight into the way sound "feels." Soon he had set up a way to speak into a machine and have the vibrations of his voice etched in a sheet of tinfoil. When the tinfoil was played back, he heard his own voice. The first words he spoke were the poem "Mary Had a Little Lamb." He called the invention a phonograph.

Edison traveled to newspaper offices in New York City. He was featured in *Scientific American*. He became world-famous and was dubbed "The Wizard of Menlo Park."

Despite all the buzz about his phonograph, Edison's attentions were focused elsewhere. He wanted to light up the world.

Although Alexander Graham Bell invented the telephone, Thomas Edison's improvements made it a device for long-distance communication.

Lights, Camera, Action!

In the 1880s, homes were lit using gas lamps, which were dirty, smelly, and dangerous. Electricity sent to a lamp produced ARC light—so bright it was

Edison's invention of the phonograph made him famous.

useless in homes. Equally useless were the era's electric lightbulbs, which lasted only a few minutes. Edison developed cotton filament covered by carbon. It burned brightly for hours. On New Year's Eve 1879, thousands of reporters and spectators trekked from the Menlo Park train station to Edison's laboratory. Their path was lit by streetlights. Every window in his lab brightly displayed his lightbulbs.

Lightbulbs gave people a reason to install electric power in their homes and businesses. In 1882, Edison built a power plant using coal-powered generators in New York City. Electricity was sent along low-voltage power lines that ran underground from the plant to people's homes.

While his invention of the lightbulb was a huge success, Edison was envisioning ways to revolutionize other businesses, such as the entertainment industry. In 1888, Edison met with photographer Eadweard

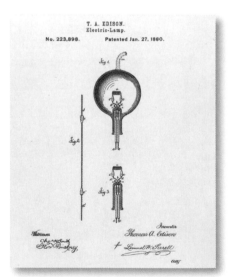

In 1880, Edison applied for a patent for his lightbulb—an invention that literally lit up the world.

Muybridge. Muybridge took action photos of animals—shots of them running or jumping. Each photo was taken a split second after the previous one. Spinning the pictures inside a viewer gave a sense of motion. Edison was inspired to invent a motion picture camera. That October, he filed a patent for a device that would "do for the eye what the phonograph does for the ear."[3]

He called it a "kinetoscope," using the Greek words *kineto*, meaning "movement," and *skopos*, meaning "to watch." By 1891, kinetoscope booths were showing movies to customers for a nickel. People lined up to watch short movies of people or animals doing different things. Soon, Edison employees suggested he project the images onto a screen. He was worried it would ruin his kinetoscope business, but eventually he went along with the idea. Crowds of people could now watch each showing.

By then, Edison music machines were playing the wax cylinders (and later records) that were developed by other people. The Edison Company even created one of the first movies to tell a story with 1903's *The Great Train Robbery*.

Not every idea he had was a success. Edison spent millions of dollars and years of his life on an unsuccessful iron ore business. He

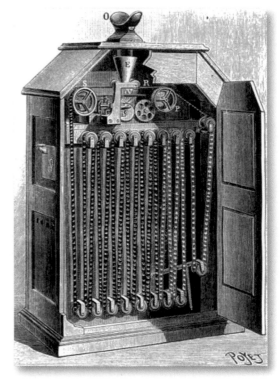

The kinetoscope allowed a single viewer to watch a short movie. It would soon be replaced by movie projectors that let audiences enjoy movies together.

17

This Tesla coil is shown discharging a burst of electricity known as a brush discharge.

championed direct current, which only worked when its noisy power plant was in the neighborhood. Nikola Tesla wanted to change that. Tesla worked in Edison's New Jersey lab as an electrical engineer. He tried to convince his boss that alternating current was more efficient than direct current. Although he failed to change Edison's mind, Tesla would invent the Tesla coil in 1891. It would be used in early television sets and radios (something Tesla had a hand in inventing, as well).

Alternating current could deliver electricity to homes many miles away. Tesla would also develop an alternating current system, which he sold to Edison's rival, George Westinghouse in 1888.

Edison often said that he didn't have 10,000 failures, just 10,000 experiments that were useful because they taught him how something *didn't* work. One of his last big failures was his attempt to power an automobile with electricity.

Edison Invents the Music Business

Imagine wanting to hear your favorite song in the 1880s. To do so, you would need to play an instrument or know someone who did. That's because songs were only on sheet music. A musician had to translate those written notes into sound.

Edison's phonograph changed that. Although it took years before popular music was recorded, when it finally happened, a booming industry was created. For the first time, musicians, singers, and composers could preserve their work. We will never know how composer Franz Schubert sounded when he played his pieces. But we can listen to Edward Elgar from 1914.

Edison recorded hundreds of musicians, singers, and actors in his West Orange studio. The brand-new business of popular music got its start there. By the 1920s, music was played over the radio and listening to music became a popular pastime in most households.

An Edison phonograph machine

Henry Ford's first car looked more like a baby carriage than an automobile. With a top speed of 20 miles per hour, this Quadricycle was powered by a two-cylinder, four-horsepower engine.

Human Machines

Henry Ford was 38 years old when he won the race that changed his life. Few expected him to win. And not even Henry imagined he would someday become the millionaire owner of the world's most successful car company.

In 1896, he had proudly shown off his Quadricycle. Featuring a pair of bicycles connected by a seat, it looked more like a baby carriage than a car. Although there was one breakdown due to from a faulty spring, the ride was considered a success. After selling the Quadricycle for $200, Ford got to work on his second car. Sporting high wheels, brass lamps, and a padded bench seat, his next invention was more like a car. With funding from people like businessman William Murphy, Ford founded the Detroit Automobile Company to sell them. It failed. So did his second car company.

In 1901, Ford challenged Alexander Winton to a race or a "sweepstakes." The man was the United States' top racer and the wealthy founder of Winton Motor Carriage Company. Ford was unknown. He wasn't a trained racecar driver. He also had nothing to lose.

Eight thousand people watched the competition at the Detroit Driving Club. Ford had trouble controlling his car on the curves and quickly fell behind. On the seventh lap, smoke billowed from Winton's car. Ford roared past. "Many of us believe if Henry Ford hadn't won that race, he might not have been able to raise the money to finally build Ford Motor Company," Edsel Ford II, great-grandson of Henry Ford, told *Automotive News.*[1]

For years, Henry Ford worked full time. Building cars was an expensive hobby. Finally, with $1,000 in prize money and the world's attention, he was able to start the Ford Motor Company.

Beginnings

Henry Ford was born on July 30, 1863. He was the first child of William and Mary Litogot Ford. Born near Dearborn, Michigan, Henry came of age on the family farm. Exposed to the brutally hard work, he imagined creating machines that would make life easier. His mother taught him how to read, while he taught himself how to repair farm equipment. In school, Henry barely made it to eighth grade.

At 16, the future car man walked nine miles to Detroit. There he began an apprenticeship at a Detroit machine shop. Later, he repaired steam engines at the Detroit Dry Dock Company.

Using steam as a power source helped modernize the 1800s. When water is heated to a boil, it produces steam. As it does so, it expands. The expansion

Henry Ford understood the machines of the past but hoped to build the machines of the future. This made Detroit Dry Dock the perfect place for the teenaged Henry to work.

creates tremendous energy. Long viewed as a potential power source, steam wasn't really harnessed until the early nineteenth century. Richard Trevithick constructed a full-sized steam engine in 1801, and Robert Fulton used a steam engine on a passenger ship six years later. The first successful steam locomotive operated in Wales in 1804; steam turbines were adopted in 1831.

Richard Trevithick's construction of this full-sized steam engine in the early 1800s led to engines that would soon power trains across the United States.

The engines Henry Ford repaired were powered by a jet of steam that turned a turbine. Even today some of our electricity is provided by steam-powered turbines. Yet, Henry saw steam engines as part of the past. At Detroit Dry Dock, he was introduced to the future. There he saw his first internal combustion engine.

Gasoline-powered engines were developed in the mid-1800s by French inventors Jean Joseph Étienne Lenoir and Alphonse Beau de Rochas. They were perfected by others, including Nikolaus A. Otto, who built a four-stroke engine, and Sir Dugald Clerk, who constructed the two-stroke.

In both types, a spark plug ignites fuel when it is released into a cylinder. The combustion forces a piston to move. The piston is connected by a rod to other devices, and these moving parts transfer movement to, say, wheels on a car or a blade on a lawn mower. In a four-stroke engine, the piston goes up-down, up-down for each spark

For years, Clara Jane Ford was one of the few people who believed in her husband Henry's dreams.

from the spark plug. In a two-stroke engine, the piston only goes up-down for each spark.

In the 1880s, Gottlieb Daimler developed the earliest versions of the internal combustion, gas-powered engine. Injected through a carburetor, gasoline fueled Daimler's four-stroke engine. This would be the engine of the future. But it would take almost a decade before Henry Ford realized this.

Meanwhile, on April 11, 1888, Ford married Clara Jane Bryant. Although his father gave him a farm as a wedding present, Henry soon returned to Detroit. In 1891, he took a job at Thomas Edison's Detroit Illuminating Company and became its chief engineer two years later. During his free time, he worked on machines. He and Clara waited five years to have children. This was unusual in the 1800s, but Henry was focused on work. They would have just one child, a boy named Edsel, who was born in 1893.

Car Man

When Henry founded Ford Motor Company in 1903, he imagined a different type of car. At the time, cars were toys for the rich. They were fancy, with complicated engines, fine leather seats, and brass plating. Ford wanted to make cars for people like his parents. Cars built for rough dirt roads. Cars that were easy to fix. And most importantly, cars that they could afford.

"He wanted to help people, and we as young men in the shop looked up to that," one of the company's first workers explained. "We could see that

Mr. Ford's mind went to the farmer and the mechanic and to the people who lived in the [countryside]."[2]

Ford assigned a letter to each car his company created. Most didn't work well. Some cost too much. He'd almost gone through the alphabet when the car he called perfect was created. In 1908, his company began producing the Model T. It was a huge success. Five years later, tens of thousands of Model Ts were on the road. Henry Ford was a millionaire. But it wasn't enough.

Skilled craftspeople built the car by working around it. It was very slow. So, instead of having his workers go to the car, Ford had the car go to them. His assembly line began over the winter of 1913.

Meat factories inspired his

At Ford Motor Company, Henry Ford started with the Model A and had almost worked his way through the alphabet before developing the Model T.

assembly line. There, animals traveled down a row of workers, who stood in place, slicing and cutting sections according to their position. On the assembly line, conveyor belts bring the car to each worker, who adds only one or a few pieces to the car. As the car moves down the line to different workers, more parts are added. Every task is simple. Workers do one thing, over and over. They don't just work on machines. In many ways, they *become* the machine. Cars that once took 12 hours to build could be assembled in just 90 minutes.

Introduced in 1913, the assembly line sped up production while making many workers feel like part of the machinery.

It was incredibly efficient. It was also incredibly boring. Ford spent millions of dollars training workers, and many of them would quit. This gave him a new problem to solve.

In 1914, he doubled workers' wages. He also reduced their hours. Instead of working ten hours a day, they worked eight. Instead of earning a little over two dollars a day, they earned five.

Businesspeople criticized these new working conditions. Most of them thought he'd fail. Two of his partners successfully sued him because he was putting money into the plant and workers instead of returning it to investors. Ford explained, "The only thing that makes anything not sell is because the price is too high . . . every time you reduce the price of the car without reducing the quality, you increase the possible number of purchasers." The more cars they could sell, the more profit they would earn. Henry wanted "to force the price of the car down as fast as production would permit, and give the benefits to users and laborers, with resulting surprisingly enormous benefits to ourselves."[3]

The "enormous benefit" for Ford was great wealth. He became one of the richest people in the world. In 1920, the Ford Motor Company sold four million Model Ts. The car cost just $440—a price that many people could afford.

Although he rarely gave credit to others, he easily credited one man with his success: Thomas Edison.

Ford, Studebaker, DeLorean . . . Tesla

In the early part of the 20th century, there were dozens of car companies. By the 1950s, there were just a handful. Today, US auto manufacturers are often called "The Big Three." These are Ford, General Motors, and Chrysler (now Stellantis).

Like the Ford Motor Company, the Packard and Studebaker were named after their founders. So was the DeLorean. Founded by the youngest executive in GM history, John DeLorean, the car he produced in the 1970s was famous for its gullwing doors and stainless steel body. By 1985, the company was out of business and already a punchline when the car was used as a time travel device in the 1985 film, *Back to the Future*.

With his insistence on a new type of factory and new type of car, many see Elon Musk as the twenty-first-century's Henry Ford. Although his Tesla automobiles began as very expensive electric cars, Musk began producing a lower-priced version in 2017. When Ford began his assembly line, he was producing over 7,000 cars a week. Musk has struggled to reach 5,000. Worse, his "low-cost" car averages over $50,000. Unlike Ford, he did not name his company after himself. Instead, he honored inventor Nikola Tesla.

Elon Musk has struggled to turn his Tesla autos into the type of low-cost, everyday car that Ford made famous.

Thomas Edison's struggle building an electric-powered car (inset) was one reason he encouraged Henry Ford's pursuit of a gas-powered one. The two became close friends and were even neighbors in Florida.

Friends and Neighbors

Thomas Edison was stumped. In the 1890s, he was world famous. People demanded Edison products even for things he didn't invent. They were convinced anything with his name on it was the best.

Not every invention was a success, and even successful ones were the result of many, many attempts. He succeeded because he wasn't afraid to fail. When he arrived at Edison Illuminating Company's New York convention, he was failing spectacularly. It was the late nineteenth century, but he was focused on a technology that wouldn't take off until the twenty-first century. Edison was working on an electric car.

The car's battery was the challenge. It needed enough juice to power a car, but so far all the batteries he developed were so heavy the car couldn't move.

During a convention dinner, Edison remembered, the head of his Detroit office, Alex Dow, told him, "over there's a young fellow who made a gas car." Edison said, "That interested me because I was giving thought to the improvement of the electric car by designing a new type of battery. I had him come over and sit next to me and quizzed him. He drew sketches for me and I was very impressed. I told him to keep at it and he did."[1]

The young man was Henry Ford. Decades later, he was certain the conversation had changed his life. "Mr. Edison listened to me very patiently. Then he banged a fist on the table and said, 'Young man, that's the thing. Your car is self-contained—no boiler, no heavy battery, no smoke or steam. Keep at it.'

"You can imagine how excited I was, the man who knew most about electricity in the world—my boyhood idol—telling me my car was better than an electric car."[2]

Besides his wife, Clara, Ford said that Edison was the only person who told him that his dream was possible. At the time, Ford needed advice. Not long after, Edison would need a friend.

Be My Neighbor

Edison's wife, Mary, had been ill throughout their marriage. In 1884, she died.

The loss almost broke Edison. Even as her illness worsened, he'd remained in Wyoming, away from home. His assistant urged him to return as soon as possible. Instead, Edison remained out west for three more weeks.

Not long after Mary's death, he left the boys with her mother and traveled with 12-year-old Marion to the International Electrical Exhibition. Later, he reconnected with a longtime friend, former telegraph operator Ezra Gilliland. The two formed a partnership, and in 1885 they took a road trip to Florida. There in the Gulfside town of Fort Myers, Edison bought 13 acres beside the Caloosahatchee River for $2,750. He gave half to Gilliland. Perhaps the inventor felt he owed it to his partner, because that summer Gilliland had introduced him to Mina Miller.

It was love at first sight. Writing in his diary, Edison admitted, "Got thinking about Mina, and come near to being run over by a street car."[3]

Unlike Mary, who'd come from a poor family, Mina was the sophisticated daughter of a millionaire inventor. She was also 19, while Edison was nearly 40. To keep their conversations private, he taught her Morse code. They would tap messages onto each other's hands. One day Edison tapped out, "Will you marry me?" She said yes.

Bright, sophisticated, and pretty, Mina Miller easily bridged the 20-year age gap between herself and her future husband, Thomas Edison.

The couple moved into a 23-room mansion in West Orange, New Jersey, where Edison oversaw the construction of a much larger lab. The couple would have three children: Madeleine, Charles, and Theodore.

By then, Thomas and Gilliland had had a falling out. His friend had taken over the sales end of the business. He convinced Edison that a company paying $500,000 for rights to sell the phonograph was the best possible deal. What he didn't tell Edison was that he'd made another $250,000 on the side. When Edison learned about this, he tore up the contract with the company and ended his partnership with Gilliland. It was also the end of their friendship. Edison even had the water lines cut to his friend's Fort Myers house. In 1916, Ford purchased the property. When he did, two of the world's richest men became next-door neighbors.

The pair also spent time together on summer camping trips. Along with wealthy tire manufacturer Harvey Firestone and naturalist John Burroughs, they made regular summer trips between 1915 and 1924. The group called themselves the Vagabonds, traveling to upstate New York,

Summer camping trips let Ford and Edison enjoy nature along with all the comforts of home. Here Ford watches his fishing line while Thomas Edison looks on beside him with friends, such as millionaire tire manufacturer Harvey Firestone.

West Virginia, and other states in the South. Their excursions were far from most people's idea of camping trips. Cars carried cooks and equipment, while the Ford Motor Company provided photographers using Edison movie cameras. During the 1919 trip, some 50 vehicles took part, including a kitchen camping car with a gasoline stove and built-in icebox.

For years Edison had ignored his health problems. By the late 1920s, stomach issues kept him from eating regular meals. He often had little except for milk. In 1931, at the age of 84, he died. A doctor used a test tube to hold the inventor's last breath. His son Charles later sent it to Henry Ford.

Florida Real Estate

Thomas Edison started trends in more than music and movies. He also started them in real estate. When he bought land in Fort Myers, Florida, a little over 300 people lived there. Today, more than 80,000 call it home, with many more visitors passing through every day. When Edison Park was developed in the 1920s, it was one of many places in the state offering new homes and a winter retreat. Thanks in part to Ford, autos were numerous. Railroads reached all the way to Key West. And a 20-year-old company president named James Draper Newton became friends with Ford and Edison as he built up the area around their homes.

   The good times did not last. The Great Depression and the lax building standards of the time led to a collapse in the Florida housing market. In 1947, Edison's widow gave their Florida home to the city of Fort Myers. Today, hundreds of thousands of people arrive every year to tour the five buildings, which include a museum of his inventions.

Now a popular tourist attraction, the stately Edison home in Fort Myers, Florida, once welcomed millionaires.

In 1935, Henry Ford was wealthy beyond his wildest dreams. He'd also lost his best friend, Thomas Edison. Meanwhile, as the Great Depression wore on, fewer people had enough money to buy new cars.

Remembrance

Presidents often lie in state, in an open coffin, at the US Capitol. Thomas Edison had similar honors. For two days and three nights, thousands of people traveled to his lab in West Orange, where the inventor's body lay. On the third night, people across the United States tuned in to radio broadcasts. They were told to shut off their lights. For minutes, darkness swept the country. It was a tribute to the man who had brought light to the world.

In 1947, Henry Ford died. Again the country mourned a man who had changed their lives. One hundred thousand people formed a line over a mile long to pay their respects as he lay in state in Greenfield Village, Michigan. By then, most homes had electricity and lights, and most people owned cars.

Despite failures and losses, Ford and Edison stuck to their dreams. They encouraged each other and offered a helping hand when it was needed. Although world famous, neither man had a large circle of friends. That made their connection even more special. Both lived long enough to see technology alter their inventions past their own understanding. And despite their enormous wealth, both were happiest at work.

On many of their summer camping trips, Edison and Ford were joined by naturalist John Burroughs (center)—a pioneer in the movement to preserve the country's natural resources.

Today cars, recorded sound, and many other technologies are being altered by the digital world. Music and movies exist as coded data on hard drives. Cars are so complex they require special computers and software to repair them. And most inventors will have spent close to 20 years in school.

Although both men had flaws and outdated views on the world, Edison and Ford contributed essential inventions and innovations to modern society. And they could always count on each other. In today's world of virtual friends and hundreds of acquaintances, it is a reminder of the value in having one best friend.

Ford, Edison, and Firestone formed a partnership in Florida. The Edison Botanic Research Corporation focused unsuccessfully on developing US rubber, which was in great demand for tires, among other things.

No matter how much money they made, both Ford and Edison seemed happiest working with their hands—even when the challenge was how to saw a tree.

Edison and Ford's love for work also followed them to their Fort Myers homes. Today, the Edison and Ford Winter Estates still house Edison's laboratory and a museum featuring various Ford car models. Their love of nature is also present at the estates with botanical gardens open to the public 363 days a year.

Going Electric

By 2019, electric cars had become an expected option on the marketplace. In the densely packed cities of China and Europe, the vehicles soon will be mandatory. Gas-powered vehicles might disappear in many parts of the world. Yet, despite billions of dollars spent developing them, the batteries these cars rely on still only allow travel of about 300 miles without recharging. It takes far longer to charge the batteries than to fill a gas tank. Electric vehicles are also impractical for long-distance road trips or package deliveries. This is one reason that currently, fewer than five percent of all the new cars bought in the world were electric.

Yet, Edison was ahead of his time. The nickel-iron battery he hoped to develop for cars was soon fitted for other uses. It would be used in everything from forklifts to trains. It became one of his most successful inventions and is still in use today because of its long life. We can only imagine what Edison and Ford would think of all the vehicles that are "going electric."

More than one hundred years after Thomas Edison's struggles with electric cars, the vehicles are growing in popularity. Charging stations like this one offer a substitute for gas stations.

1847   Thomas Alva Edison is born on February 11 in Milan, Ohio, to Samuel and Nancy Edison. He is their seventh and youngest child.

1854   The Edison family moves to Port Huron, Michigan.

1859   Thomas takes his first job selling newspapers on a train.

1862   Thomas begins publishing the *Weekly Herald*.

1863   Having taught himself Morse code, Thomas takes a job as a telegraph operator. He works in press offices around the country.

           On July 30, Henry Ford is born to William and Mary Litogot Ford in Dearborn, Michigan.

1868   Not long after settling in Boston, Massachusetts, Thomas earns his first patent for an electric vote recorder. The device is a flop.

1871   Thomas Edison buys a factory in Newark, New Jersey, and transforms it into a workshop and manufacturing facility. He marries Mary Stillwell on Christmas Day.

1874   Edison develops the quadruplex telegraph system; he sells it for $40,000 to Western Union.

1876   Edison relocates to the Invention Factory, a 34-acre site in Menlo Park that includes large manufacturing facilities and laboratories. Alexander Graham Bell invents the telephone.

1877   Edison invents the phonograph.

1879   The first public demonstration of Edison's incandescent lightbulb takes place on October 21.

1880   At 16, Henry moves to Detroit, Michigan, and becomes an apprentice in a machine shop.

1882   Edison's Pearl Street electric power plant, the first in the world, opens.

1884	Mary Edison dies of typhoid fever.
1886	Edison marries Mina Miller, the daughter of a successful inventor.
1888	Ford marries Clara Jane Bryant.
1891	Ford is hired at Edison's Detroit Illuminating Company. He eventually becomes chief engineer. During his free time he builds a Quadricycle, his first car.
	Edison invents a moving picture machine--the kinetoscope.
1896	Edison and Ford meet for the first time.
1903	Edison produces *The Great Train Robbery*, one of the first films to tell a story.
	Ford founds the Ford Motor Company.
1908	The Ford Motor Company introduces the Model T. It will become the best-selling car in the world.
1913	Henry Ford introduces the assembly line. It allows cars to be made much faster.
1914	Because bored and exhausted workers keep quitting, Ford creates the five-dollar day, paying twice as much as other factories.
	Edison's research facility in West Orange, New Jersey, burns down.
1916	Ford moves next door to Edison.
1931	Thomas Edison dies at the age of 84.
1946	Mina Edison dies.
1947	Henry Ford dies.

Chapter 1. Unlikely Savior

1. Newton, James Draper. *Uncommon Friends: Life with Thomas Edison, Henry Ford, Harvey Firestone, Alexis Carrel, and Charles Lindbergh* (New York: Houghton Mifflin Harcourt, 1987), p. 16.

2. "Edison Sees His Vast Plant Burn," *The New York Times*, December 10, 1914, p. 1. https://timesmachine.nytimes.com/timesmachine/1914/12/10/100121297.pdf

3. Newton, p. 7.

4. Ibid., p. 16.

5. Wolkomir, Richard, and Joyce Wolkomir. "Mr. Edison Takes a Holiday." *Smithsonian*, December 1999, p. 136.

Chapter 2. The Wizard

1. McAuliffe, Kathleen. "The Undiscovered World of Thomas Edison." *The Atlantic*, December 1995, p. 80.

2. Bedi, Joyce. "Thomas Edison's Inventive Life." National Museum of American History, April 18, 2004. https://invention.si.edu/thomas-edisons-inventive-life

3. "Origins of Motion Pictures," Library of Congress. https://www.loc.gov/collections/edison-company-motion-pictures-and-sound-recordings/articles-and-essays/history-of-edison-motion-pictures/origins-of-motion-pictures/

Chapter 3. Human Machines

1. Martinez, Michael. "Holy Grail: Edsel Ford II Holds Out Hope that Someone Will Find His Great-grandfather's Life-changing Prize," *Automotive News*, January 29, 2018, p. 1.
2. Colt, Sarah. "Henry Ford: The Most Influential Innovator of the 20th Century." *American Experience*. PBS, January 29, 2013. https://www-tc.pbs.org/wgbh/americanexperience/media/pdf/transcript/henryford_transcript.pdf
3. Rose, Cynthia, ed. "Henry Ford's Business Philosophy." *American Decades Primary Sources*. Vol. 2: 1910–1919. Detroit: Gale. 2004, pp. 98–102.

Chapter 4. Friends and Neighbors

1. Newton, James Draper. *Uncommon Friends: Life with Thomas Edison, Henry Ford, Harvey Firestone, Alexis Carrel, and Charles Lindbergh* (New York: Houghton Mifflin Harcourt, 1987), p. 9.
4. Ibid., pp. 9–10.
5. Ferrari, Michelle. "Edison: The Wizard of Menlo Park." *American Experience*. PBS, January 27, 2015.

Books

Gregory, Josh, *Henry Ford: Father of the Auto Industry*. New York: Children's Press, 2014.

Hamen, Susan E., *Who Invented the Light Bulb?: Edison vs. Swan*. Minneapolis: Lerner Publications, 2018.

Kenney, Karen Latchana. *Who Invented the Movie Camera?: Edison vs. Friese-Greene*. Minneapolis: Lerner Publications, 2018.

Kramer, Barbara. *Thomas Edison*. Washington, D.C.: National Geographic, 2014.

Krieg, Katherine. *Thomas Edison: World-changing Inventor*. Minneapolis: Core Library, 2015.

McDowell, Pamela. *Henry Ford*. New York: AV² by Weigl, 2014.

Slade, Suzanne. *The Inventor's Secret: What Thomas Edison Told Henry Ford*. Watertown, MA: Charlesbridge, 2015.

Works Consulted

Anderson, Amy. "Legacy of Light: Thomas Edison Turned Countless Failures into a Lifetime of Success." *Success*. September 2009.

Bedi, Joyce. "Thomas Edison's Inventive Life," Smithsonian Natural Museum of American History. April 18, 2004. https://invention.si.edu/thomas-edisons-inventive-life

Carpenter, Frank G. "An Interview with Thomas Edison in His Laboratory." *The Salt Lake Herald*. November 8, 1891. https://www.newspapers.com/title_1618/the_salt_lake_herald/

Colt, Sarah. "Henry Ford: The Most Influential Innovator of the 20th Century." *American Experience*. PBS. January 29, 2013. https://www-tc.pbs.org/wgbh/americanexperience/media/pdf/transcript/henryford_transcript.pdf

D'Amico, Esther. "'Invention Factory' Revisited." *Chemical Week*. May 29, 1996.

"Edison: Man of the Millennium." *Newsweek*. May 18, 1998.

"Edison Quits Record Biz." *Music Trades*. November. 2004.

"Edison Sees His Vast Plant Burn." *The New York Times*. December 10, 1914. https://timesmachine.nytimes.com/timesmachine/1914/12/10/100121297.pdf

Eisman, Alberta. "Thomas Edison's Florida." *The New York Times*. June 24, 1990. https://www.nytimes.com/1990/06/24/travel/thomas-edison-s-florida.html

Ferrari, Michelle. "Edison: The Wizard of Menlo Park." *American Experience*. PBS. January 27, 2015.

Finn, Bernard D. "Thomas Alva Edison after Forty: The Challenge of Success." *USA Today* [supplement]. July 1994.

Friess, Steve, and Adeel Hassan. "Why Did a Mayor Try to Play Down Henry Ford's (Well-Known) Dark Side?" *The New York Times*. February 3, 2019.

"Henry Ford and the Telegraph." *Michigan History Magazine*. July–August 2017.

Labowitz, Sarah. "Factory Safety and Labor Protections; The Difference between the Triangle Shirtwaist Factory Fire and Rana Plaza." NYU/Stern. March 25, 2016. https://bhr.stern.nyu.edu/blogs/105th-anniversary-triangle-shirtwaist

Majeski, Brian T. "Henry Ford and Steve Jobs . . . Retail Revolutionaries." *Music Trades*. August 2015.

Marshall, Tom. "Text to Text—Bangladesh Factory Safety and the Triangle Shirtwaist Fire," *The New York Times* (Learning Blogs). April 8, 2014. https://learning.blogs.nytimes.com/2014/04/08/text-to-text-bangladesh-factory-safety-and-the-triangle-shirtwaist-fire/

Martinez, Michael. "Holy Grail: Edsel Ford II Holds Out Hope that Someone Will Find His Great-grandfather's Life-changing Prize." *Automotive News*. January 29, 2018.

McAuliffe, Kathleen. "The Undiscovered World of Thomas Edison." *The Atlantic*, December 1995.

Miller, M.H. "When Michigan Was Modern." *New York Times*. September 9, 2018.

Myers, Steven III. *The Five-Dollar Day: Labor Management and Social Control in the Ford Motor Company, 1908–1921*. Albany: State University of New York Press, 1981.

Newton, James Draper. *Uncommon Friends: Life with Thomas Edison, Henry Ford, Harvey Firestone, Alexis Carrel, and Charles Lindbergh*. New York: Houghton Mifflin Harcourt, 1987.

"Origins of Motion Pictures." Library of Congress. https://www.loc.gov/collections/edison-company-motion-pictures-and-sound-recordings/articles-and-essays/history-of-edison-motion-pictures/origins-of-motion-pictures/

Pope, Eric. "$5 day: Is Henry Ford Nuts?!" *Crain's Detroit Business*. June 27, 2001.

———. "Now About This Assembly Line . . ." *Crain's Detroit Business*. June 27, 2001.

Rose, Cynthia. Ed. "Henry Ford's Business Philosophy." *American Decades Primary Sources, Vol. 2: 1910–1919*. Detroit: Gale, 2004.

"Telephone Transmitter." *Thomas A. Edison Papers*. Rutgers School of Arts and Sciences. https://edison.rutgers.edu/life-of-edison/inventions?view=article&id=541:telephone-transmitter&catid=91:inventions

"Test Tube: Edison's Last Breath, 1931." The Henry Ford Organization. https://www.thehenryford.org/collections-and-research/digital-collections/artifact/225212/

"The Vagabonds." The Henry Ford Organization. https://www.thehenryford.org/collections-and-research/digital-resources/popular-topics/the-vagabonds

Von Drehle, David. "What Bangladesh Can Learn from New York's Triangle Factory Fire," *Time*. May 2, 2013. http://ideas.time.com/2013/05/02/what-bangladesh-can-learn-from-new-yorks-triangle-factory-fire/

Wernle, Bradford. "Looking at Henry Ford the Man." *Automotive News*, February 11, 2013.

White, Timothy. "His Master's Voice: A Matter of Trust." *Billboard*, November 1, 1994.

Williams, Cynthia. "The First Lady of Fort Myers." *Fort Myers News-Press*, May 12, 2018. https://www.news-press.com/story/life/2018/05/12/first-lady-fort-myers-mina-thomas-edison-history-fors-estates/585115002/

Wolkomir, Richard, and Joyce Wolkomir. "Mr. Edison Takes a Holiday." *Smithsonian*, December 1999.

On the Internet

The Henry Ford Museum of American Innovation
https://www.thehenryford.org

PBS: Who Made America? "Henry Ford"
http://www.pbs.org/wgbh/theymadeamerica/whomade/ford_lo.html

Thomas Edison Inventions
https://sciencing.com/inventions-thomas-edison-kids-8616444.html

alternating current (AL-ter-nay-ting KUR-ent)—Electrical current that can travel long distances while changing direction many times each second.

apprentice (uh-PREN-tis)—A helper or assistant who works under a more experienced person to learn about a job or profession.

carburetor (KAR-bur-ay-tor)—A device that mixes a spray of fuel with air.

direct current (dur-EKT KUR-ent)—Electric current that flows in just one direction and can only travel a short distance.

filament (FIL-uh-munt)—A thread or wire that can conduct electricity.

optimist (OP-tih-mist)—A person who has a positive outlook about the future and how things will turn out.

patent (PAT-ent)—A legal document that prevents others from making money from an inventor's idea.

piston (PIS-tun)—A cylinder that fits inside a tube and is forced rapidly up and down.

technology (tek-NAH-luh-jee)—The practical use of knowledge, especially in industry.

turbine (TUR-byn)—A machine that uses a wheel or rotor to produce power.

Index

Batchelor, Charles 15
Bell, Alexander Graham 15, 40
Burroughs, John 31, 36

Chrysler (Stellantis) 27
Clerk, Sir Dugald 23

Daimler, Gottlieb 24
DeLorean, John 27
Detroit Dry Dock 22–23
Detroit, Michigan 7, 11–12, 21–24, 29, 40–41
Dow, Alex 29

Edison, Charles 5, 6, 31–32
Edison, Madeleine 31
Edison, Marion 14, 30
Edison, Mary (Stillwell) 14, 30–31, 40–41
Edison, Mina (Miller) 6, 30–31, 41
Edison, Nancy 11, 40
Edison, Samuel 11, 40
Edison, Theodore 31
Edison, Thomas Alva
  AC vs DC battle 18
  birth 11
  carbon button (telephone) 15
  childhood 11–12
  death 32, 35, 41
  electric car 27, 29–30, 39
  first patent 13–14
  five-dollar day 7, 26, 41
  helped by Henry Ford 7
  iron ore failure 17–18
  lightbulb 16, 40
  marriage to Mary Stillwell 15
  marriage to Mina Miller 31
  motion pictures 4, 5, 17, 41
  phonograph 15–16, 19, 31, 40
  quadruplex telegraph system 13, 40
  sound recording 5, 19
  telegraph operator 13, 30, 40
Edison, Thomas, Jr. 14
Edison, William 14
Edison Botanic Research Corporation 37

Edison Lofts 9
Edison Park 33
electrical vote recorder, invention of 13–14
Elgar, Edward 19

Firestone, Harvey 31–32, 37
Ford, Clara Jane (Bryant) 24, 30, 37, 41
Ford, Edsel 24
Ford, Edsel, II 22
Ford, Henry
  assembly line 25–26, 41
  at Detroit Illuminating company 24, 41
  birth 22, 40
  childhood 22, 40
  death 35, 41
  at Detroit Dry Dock 22–23
  helped by Thomas Edison 8, 29–30
  marriage to Clara Jane Bryant 24
  as racecar driver 21–22
Ford, Mary (Litogot) 22, 40
Ford Motor Company 22, 24–27, 32, 41
Ford, William 22, 40
Fort Myers, Florida 2, 28, 30–31, 33, 37–38
Fulton, Robert 23

gasoline-powered engines, invention of 23–24, 28
General Motors 27
Gilliland, Ezra 30–31
Grand Trunk Railroad 11–12
Great Depression 34

Halgrim, Bob 8

Israel, Paul 11

kinetoscope 17, 41

Lenoir, J. J. Étienne 23
lightbulb, invention of 16, 40

Menlo Park, New Jersey 14–16, 40
Milan, Ohio 11, 40
Miller, Mina 6, 30–31, 41
Model T 8, 25–26, 41
Morse code 12–13, 15, 31, 40
Morse, Samuel F.B. 12–13
motion picture camera, invention of 17
Murphy, William 21
Musk, Elon 27
Muybridge, Eadweard 16–17

Newton, James Draper 5–8, 33

Otto, Nikolaus A. 23

phonograph, invention of 15–16

Quadricycle 20–21, 41
quadruplex telegraph system, invention of 13–14

Rochas, Alphonse Beau de 23

Schubert, Franz 19
steam engine, invention of 22–23

telegraph, invention of 12–13
telephone, invention of 15
Tesla coil, invention of 18
Tesla, Nikola 18, 27
Trevithick, Richard 23

Vagabonds 31–32

West Orange, New Jersey 5, 7, 19, 31, 35, 41
Western Union Telegraph Company 13, 40
Westinghouse, George 18
Winton, Alexander 21–22